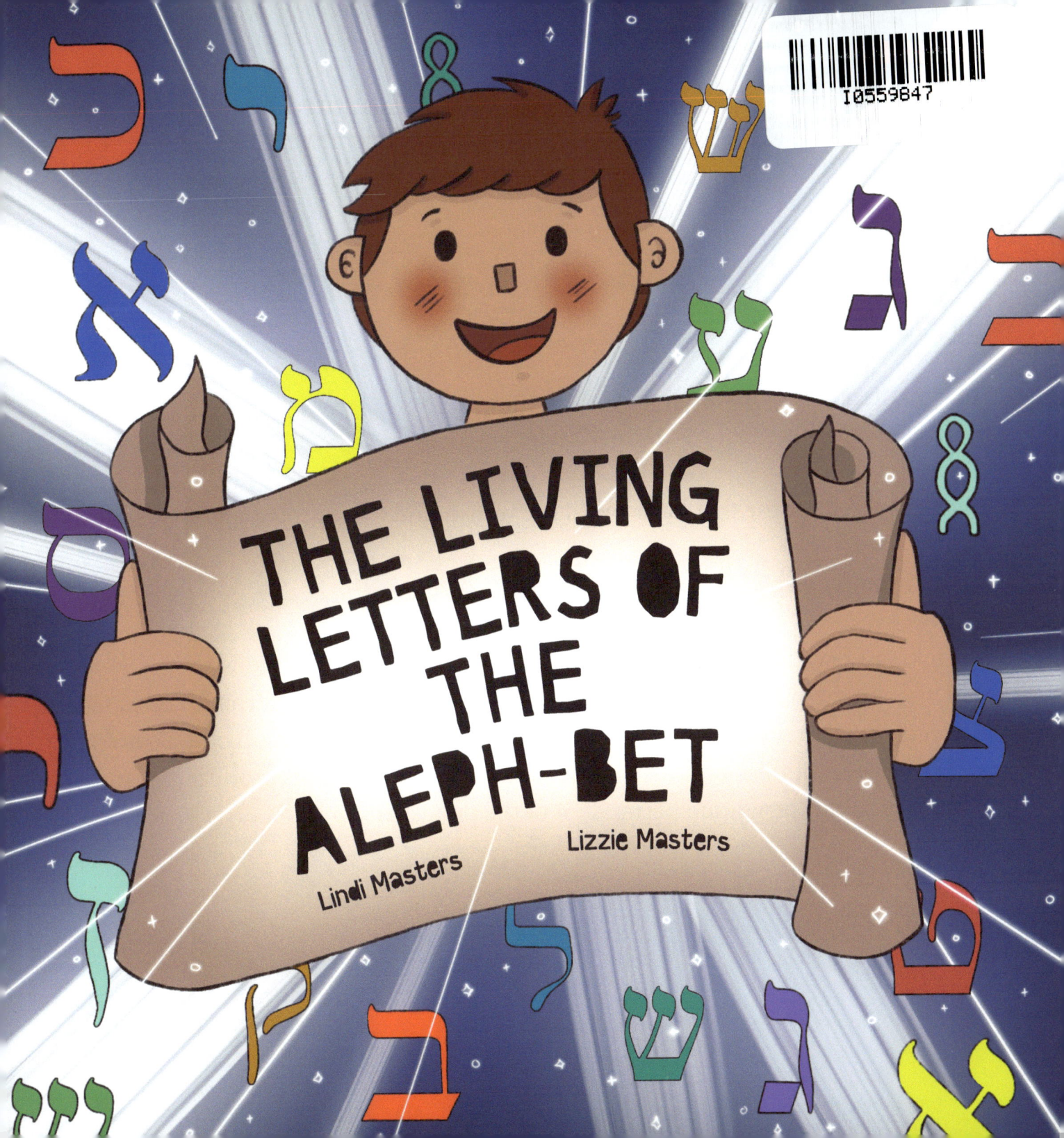

THE LIVING LETTERS OF THE ALEPH-BET

Lindi Masters

Lizzie Masters

Written by
Lindi Masters©

Illustrated by
Lizzie Masters©

Lindi Masters

Lizzie Masters

THE LIVING LETTERS OF THE ALEPH-BET

This Book Belongs to:

_____

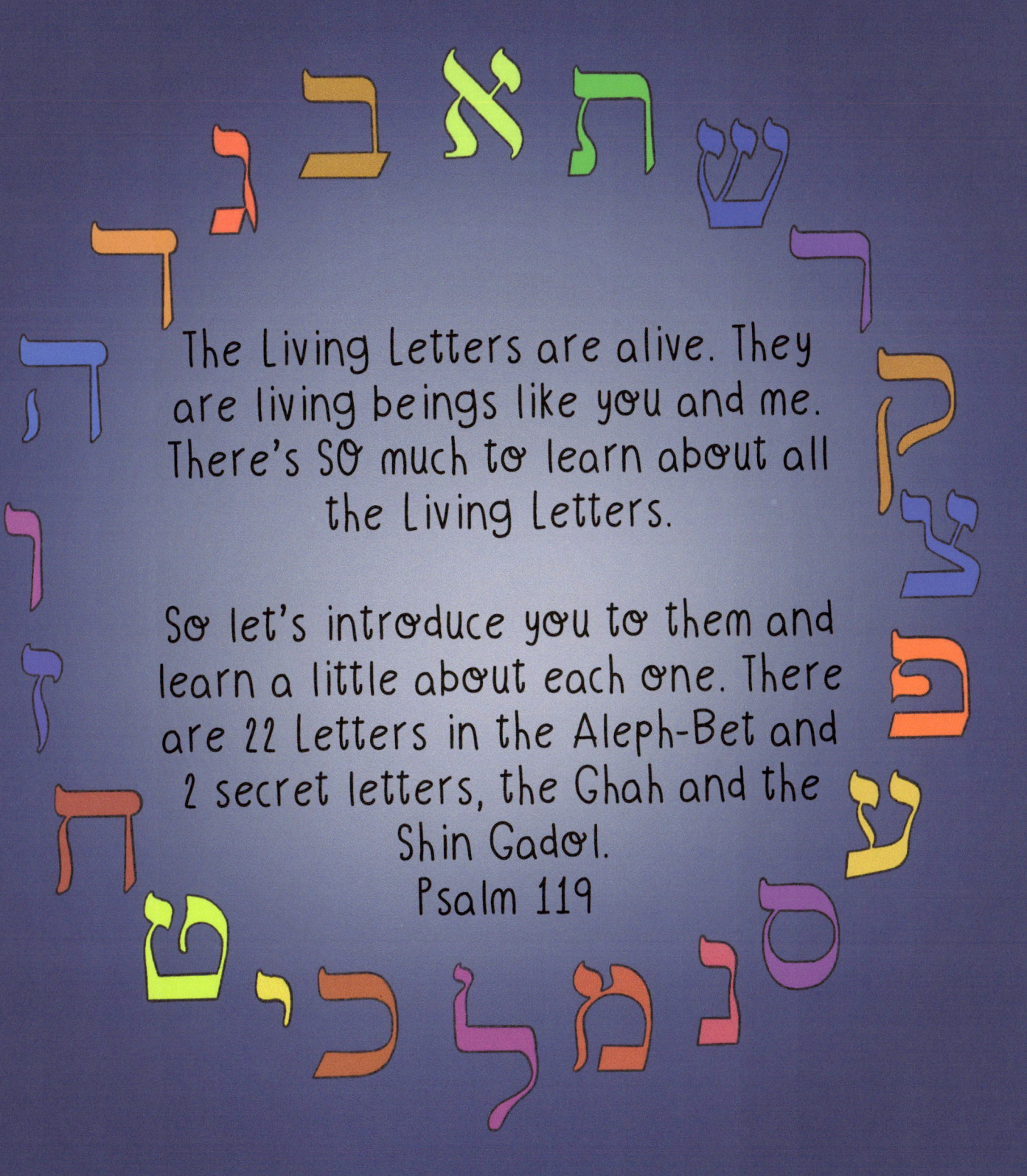

The Living Letters are alive. They are living beings like you and me. There's SO much to learn about all the Living Letters.

So let's introduce you to them and learn a little about each one. There are 22 Letters in the Aleph-Bet and 2 secret letters, the Ghah and the Shin Gadol.
Psalm 119

THE HEAVENS ABOVE

PALEO

THE EARTH BELOW

Aleph

Aleph is quiet like a whisper. Aleph connects us to Heaven from Earth. The original Hebrew, the paleo, looked like an ox. So, Aleph is strong like an ox. The number of Aleph is 1.

STRONG FOUNDATION

PALEO

Beit

Beit is like a house, the dwelling house of the Father. Beit has a strong foundation/floor. When Beit is around, we know we are in a safe place. Beit speaks and breathes. The number of Beit is 2.

PALEO

Gimel

Gimel is a camel or a foot of a running man. A Camel carries lots of supplies, like bags of money. We call Gimel the full supply. The number of Gimel is 3.

PALEO

Dalet

Dalet is a door but it is also a path or portal to all dimensions. The paleo looks like a gate. We stand at the door of our tent or gate and we wait for the full supply that comes from Gimel. They live next to each other. Gimel runs into the door of Dalet. The number of Dalet is 4.

N

W

E

S

" LOOK
BEHOLD
LOOK "

5

PALEO

Hey

Hey says Look! Behold! Hey is like the breath of Yahweh. It breathes in and out and blows the breath of Yahweh into us and into all four corners. North, East, South and West. The number of Hey is 5.

PALEO

5

6

6

CONNECT HEAVEN TO EARTH

1

N

2

W

E

4

3

S

Vav

Vav looks like a tent peg, it grabs that which comes from Heaven and secures it onto the earth. Vav has six dimensions, north, south, east and west. The other two dimensions are the Up into the Realms of the Kingdom and the Down into all of creation. It also reaches up and connects us to the tabernacle of Yahweh. The number of Vav is 6.

7

12
11
1
10
2
9
3
8
4
7
5
6

MOVES THROUGH TIME

WRITES IN MY SCROLL

PALEO

Zayin

Zayin is like a tool, that cuts. Zayin connects to time. It helps us to move through time. It helps us to uncover the things that are hidden. It takes us out of time and it opens up time, cutting into it so that we are not stuck. Zayin is also like a writer's pen, and it writes into my scroll. The number of Zayin is 7.

Chet

Chet is like a wall/boundary that divides. It leads us into the secret place. It is a secret place we have with Yahweh, where Yahweh whispers secrets to us from places of mystery. Chet is a very happy letter and the number of Chet is 8.

Tet

Tet is like a basket. It is like being wrapped and surrounded by the name of Yahweh. There is a voice that comes out of Tet that speaks and engages with us. Inside the basket are things that come from Yahweh that fill it. My scroll, the Name of Yahweh and love (Hebrew: Ahava) go into my basket. The number of Tet is 9.

Every Letter starts with a YOD

PALEO

Outstretched and Strong

10

Yod

Yod is the smallest Hebrew letter. It is like a little dot or an atom. It is the allspark that brings change. Every Hebrew letter starts with and has the Yod in it. The Paleo is like a strong arm and a hand. The number of Yod is 10.

20

PALÉO

Kaf

Kaf is like the open palm of a hand. Kaf reaches into the Heavens and brings it onto the face of the earth. It releases the knowledge of Heaven. Like an open hand we receive it and we release it into creation. The number of Kaf is 20.

30

PALEO

THE WAY

Lamed

Lamed is the tallest letter and reaches up the highest. It reaches right up into Heaven. Lamed is like a shepherd's staff that they use to pull the sheep to them and teach the sheep where to go. Lamed teaches us how to come into the things of the Kingdom. Lamed is anchored like a solid rock. Lamed guides us on the path, The Way, (Hebrew: Derekh). The number of Lamed is 30.

Mem

Mem is water. The upper waters and the lower waters. The upper waters are the secrets of Yahweh and the lower waters are the mysteries of Yahweh. The Paleo looks like a frequency or a vibration, like a reading on a machine. The number of Mem is 40.

50

Nun

Nun is like a seed planted to grow a family tree. It has your whole family in it, your mom and dad and brothers and sisters. The nun is about generations. Nun is also like a humble and faithful prince, just like you, a Son. The number of Nun is 50.

PALEO

60

PROTECTED, COVERED, SHIELDED

I AM SAFE

Samekh

Samekh is about support. Samekh means we can lean on Yahweh's support. It also means being in Yahweh's protection, being covered and shielded by Yahweh. So Samekh comes to protect you. The number of Samekh is 60.

70

PALEO

FULL SUPPLY

Ayin

Ayin is an eye. Ayin sees the mysteries and provision in our lives. Full supply comes from that fountain which is like a river that flows from Ayin. Ayin watches everything. The number of Ayin is 70.

Pey

Pey in the Paleo is like a mouth that speaks. Pey speaks and can sing into creation. The number of Pey is 80.

Tsade

Tsade looks like a man lying on his side. He is a humble man. Tsade also takes us on a journey down a path to run and search for the mysteries of Yahweh. The number of Tsade is 90.

Qof

Qof is like the sun behind time. Qof is the longest letter. Qof reaches into the secret place to find the mysteries of Yahweh. The mysteries are above the sun and behind time. The number of Qof is 100.

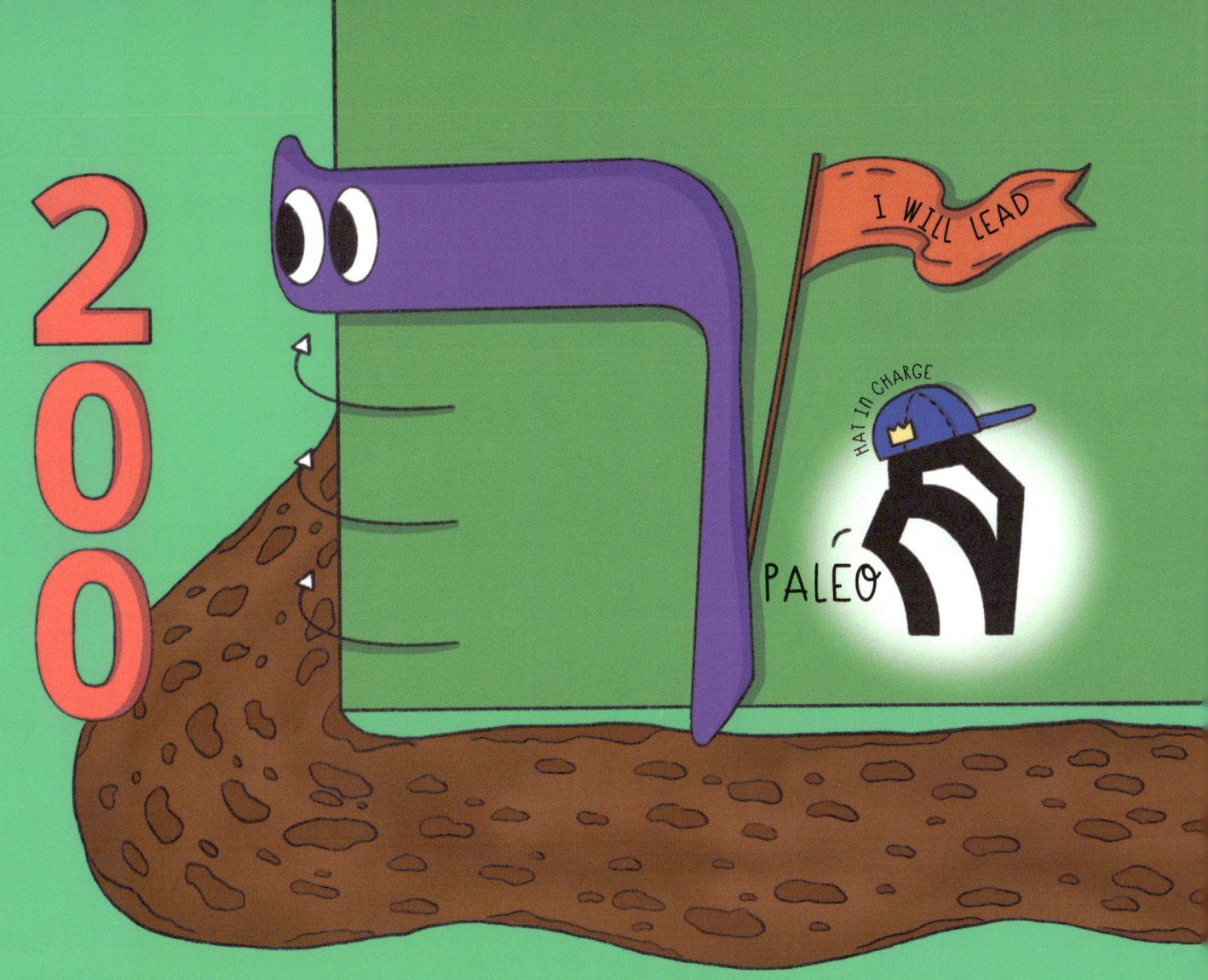

Resh

Resh has authority like a leader. Resh is the head, top or the beginning. Like the head of a man. Resh looks around the corner to see the truth. It looks around the corner to see original intent. The number of Resh is 200.

Shin

Shin in the Paleo looks like a fork sticking up. Shin grabs onto something and doesn't let go. Shin is also like a fire. When we write Yahweh's name (YOD HEY VAV HEY) we can put the shin in the middle of Yahweh's name. The three flames of the shin stand for the Father (Yahweh), the Son (Yeshua) and the Holy Spirit (Ruwach Ha Kodesh). And because the Shin sits like a crown on our head, we can put our name in the middle of Yahweh's name too. We live in the middle of Yahweh's name. The number for Shin is 300.

Tav

Tav in the Paleo looks like a cross but in the very ancient Paleo it looked like an 'x'. Tav is not the end, it is the finish line. The Alef starts the race. Tav finishes the race and starts the next race. It finishes one thing to start the next thing. Tav shows us the secret of the Ghah and points to it for us. The number for Tav is 400.

500

Ghah

Ghah is a hidden letter and is very important. Ghah can do interesting things and take us to special places. Ghah was hidden in the eye of Ayin. Ghah creates a pathway like a ladder for us and shows us how to go up into the realms of the Kingdom and bring the revelation of Heaven back into creation. The number of Ghah could be 500.

Shin Gadol

Shin Gadol is the letter that brings fire. Shin Gadol was hidden in the letter Shin. When we ascend into the Realms with Ghah, Shin Gadol helps us to see the secrets. The 3 flame Shin shows us the world that is and the 4 flame Shin Gadol shows us the world that is hidden and things that are coming. It is the fire that sits inside of us. The number for Shin Gadol could be 600.

THE LIVING LETTERS OF THE ALEPH-BET

ALEPH 1
Strong
Ox
Quiet

BEIT 2
House
Dwelling
Safe

GIMEL 3
Camel
Foot
Full Supply

DALET 4
Door
Gate
Access

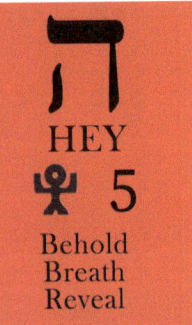

HEY 5
Behold
Breath
Reveal

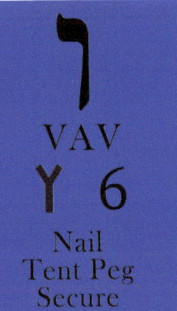

VAV 6
Nail
Tent Peg
Secure

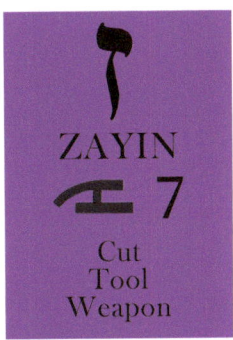

ZAYIN 7
Cut
Tool
Weapon

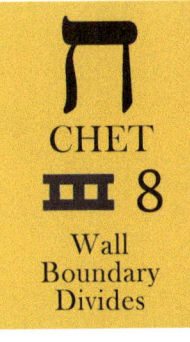

CHET 8
Wall
Boundary
Divides

TET 9
Basket
Surround
Covering

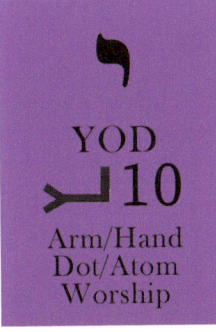

YOD 10
Arm/Hand
Dot/Atom
Worship

KAF 20
Palm
Release
To Open

LAMED 30
Shepherd
Learn/Teach
To/From

MEM 40
Water
Hidden/Secret
Vibration

NUN 50
Seed
Continue/
Increase
Life

SAMEKH 60
Support
Protect
Thorn

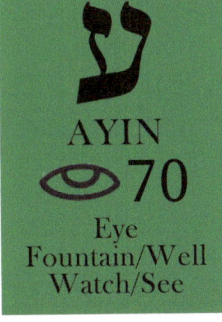

AYIN 70
Eye
Fountain/Well
Watch/See

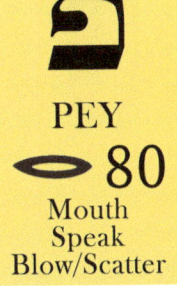

PEY 80
Mouth
Speak
Blow/Scatter

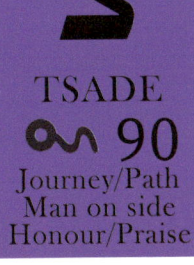

TSADE 90
Journey/Path
Man on side
Honour/Praise

QOF 100
Sun
Behind
Time

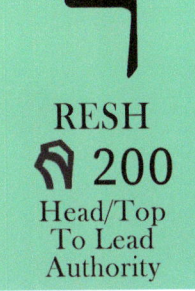

RESH 200
Head/Top
To Lead
Authority

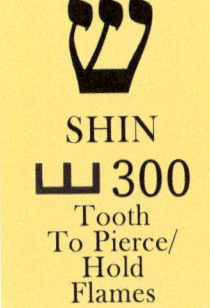

SHIN 300
Tooth
To Pierce/
Hold
Flames

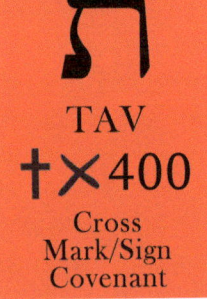

TAV 400
Cross
Mark/Sign
Covenant

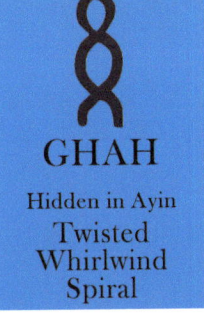

GHAH
Hidden in Ayin
Twisted
Whirlwind
Spiral

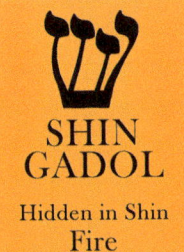

SHIN GADOL
Hidden in Shin
Fire
Secrets
Future

ZAYIN

LAMED

QOF/
QUPH

TSADE

RESH

ר

ZAYIN

ז

7

SHIN

ש

Tsade – Journey
90.an.

TSade

Uriec

NUN

ALEF OX Strength Leader

Revd

Finished

END

IS NOT

TAV
✝ 400

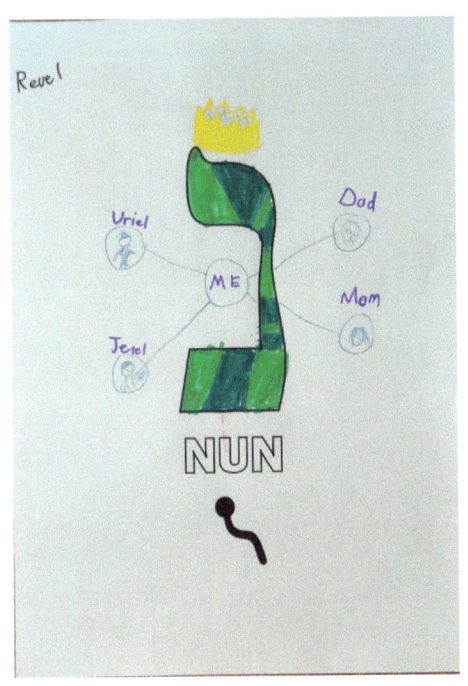

Jordan Massé USA

Josiah-Talon Massé
USA

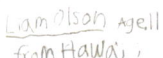

Juliette oson
Juliette Age
Hawaii 5 yr

Avigail, Age 13, Hawaii

TSADE

PA

QOF/
QUPH

Savannah Age 3
Hawaii USA

QOF/
QUPH

BEYT **BEYT** BE

Jared-NZ

PEY

אַלֶף

TSADE

mysteries

DALET

QOF/ QUPH

Secret Place

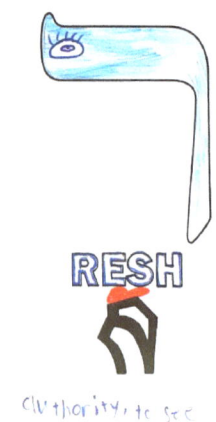

RESH

authority, to see

ALEPH

www.ingramcontent.com/pod-product-compliance
Lightning Source LLC
Chambersburg PA
CBHW041435120626
46547CB00002B/229